Bird Watching

Written by Roger Carr
Illustrated by Pat Reynolds

sundance
A Haights Cross Communications Company

Saira was watching a television show about animals.

"How can they get the television camera so close to the tiger?" she asked her dad. "It's a wild animal!"

"The man with the camera is using a blind," said Dad. "It's like a little hut, and the animals can't see him."

"I wish I had a blind so that I could get close to the birds in the backyard," said Saira. "Even when I feed them, they fly away."

"We can build a blind," said Dad. "Then the birds will come up close to you."

"How can we build a blind?" asked Saira.

"We can use the large box that the washing machine came in," said Dad.

The box was just big enough for Saira to sit in. Dad cut a doorway on one side. Then he cut a window on the other side.

"When the door is shut, the birds won't be able to see you in the box," said Dad.

5

Saira put some leaves on top of the box. Next she put some potted plants in front of it. Then she spread some bread crumbs on the ground.

She went back inside the house with Dad, and they watched from the kitchen window.

The birds sat in the trees and looked at the bread crumbs. They didn't fly down to eat them right away. First they looked around to make sure there was no danger. Then they flew down and ate the bread crumbs.

"It works!" cried Saira excitedly.

She ran outside with more bread crumbs and spread them in front of the blind. Then she crawled inside the blind and shut the door.

9

Saira looked through the window. She could see the birds in the trees. They were looking at the bread crumbs, but they didn't fly down to eat them.

Saira waited and waited and waited, but the birds did not come down to eat the bread crumbs.

It doesn't work, Saira thought to herself.

She got out of the blind and went inside.

11

"The blind doesn't work," Saira told her dad.

But when they looked out of the kitchen window, the birds were eating the bread crumbs.

"Try it again, and I'll watch from the kitchen," said Dad.

Saira spread more bread crumbs in front of the blind. Then she crawled into the blind again. Still, the birds did not come.

Dad watched from the kitchen window. He smiled to himself and then went outside.

"It's no good. It doesn't work," said Saira, as she crawled out of the blind.

"I know why it isn't working," said Dad.

Saira looked around. "Kimo!" she cried.

Dad took the cat back into the house.

Saira crawled back into the blind and
watched the birds through the window.
The birds flew out of the trees and
began to eat the bread crumbs.

Saira was so close that she could see their bright eyes and sharp beaks. She watched as they pecked the bread crumbs.

The next time, Saira took her camera.